STATES

ILLINOIS

A MyReportLinks.com Book

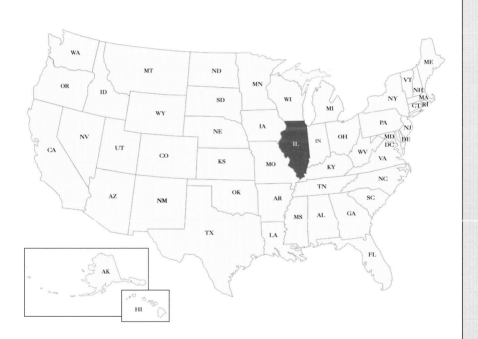

Judy Alter

MyReportLinks.com Books

an imprint of

 Enslow Publishers, Inc. **E**

Box 398, 40 Industrial Road
Berkeley Heights, NJ 07922
USA

MyReportLinks.com Books, an imprint of Enslow Publishers, Inc. MyReportLinks is a trademark of Enslow Publishers, Inc.

Library of Congress Cataloging-in-Publication Data

Alter, Judy, 1938–
    Illinois / Judy Alter.
        p. cm. — (States)
    Summary: Discusses the land and climate, economy, government, and history of the state of Illinois. Includes Internet links to Web sites.
    Includes bibliographical references and index.
    ISBN 0-7660-5111-0
    1. Illinois—Juvenile literature. [1. Illinois.] I. Title. II. States (Series : Berkeley Heights, N.J.)
F541.3 .A48 2003
977.3—dc21
                    2002003415

Printed in the United States of America

10 9 8 7 6 5 4 3 2 1

To Our Readers:
Through the purchase of this book, you and your library gain access to the Report Links that specifically back up this book.

The Publisher will provide access to the Report Links that back up this book and will keep these Report Links up to date on **www.myreportlinks.com** for three years from the book's first publication date.

We have done our best to make sure all Internet addresses in this book were active and appropriate when we went to press. However, the author and the Publisher have no control over, and assume no liability for, the material available on those Internet sites or on other Web sites they may link to.

The usage of the MyReportLinks.com Books Web site is subject to the terms and conditions stated on the Usage Policy Statement on **www.myreportlinks.com**.

In the future, a password may be required to access the Report Links that back up this book. The password is found on the bottom of page 4 of this book.

Any comments or suggestions can be sent by e-mail to comments@myreportlinks.com or to the address on the back cover.

Photo Credits: Abraham Lincoln Historical Digitization Project, p. 35; © Corel Corporation, p. 3; © 1999 Photodisc, pp. 15, 22, 27; © 2001 Robesus, Inc., p. 10; Chicago Historical Society, pp. 38, 40, 42; Chicago Public Library, pp. 11, 28; Department of the Interior, p. 33; *Dictionary of American Portraits*, Dover Publications, Inc., © 1967, p. 13; Enslow Publishers, Inc., pp. 1, 21; Illinois Historic Preservation Agency, pp. 17, 18; Library of Congress, p. 3 (Constitution); MyReportLinks.com Books, p. 4; Springfield, Illinois Convention and Visitor's Bureau, p. 28; Swarthmore College, p. 41; The Black Press: Soldiers Without Swords, PBS, p. 30; The Illinois Labor History Society, p. 26; University of Kansas, p. 24; White House Photo, p. 37.

Cover Photo: © 1999 PhotoDisc, Inc.

Cover Description: The Chicago skyline at dusk.

Contents

MyReportLinks.com Books
Great Books, Great Links, Great for Research!

MyReportLinks.com Books present the information you need to learn about your report subject. In addition, they show you where to go on the Internet for more information. The pre-evaluated Report Links that back up this book are kept up to date on **www.myreportlinks.com**. With the purchase of a MyReportLinks.com Books title, you and your library gain access to the Report Links that specifically back up that book. The Report Links save hours of research time and link to dozens—even hundreds—of Web sites, source documents, and photos related to your report topic.

Please see "To Our Readers" on the Copyright page for important information about this book, the MyReportLinks.com Books Web site, and the Report Links that back up this book.

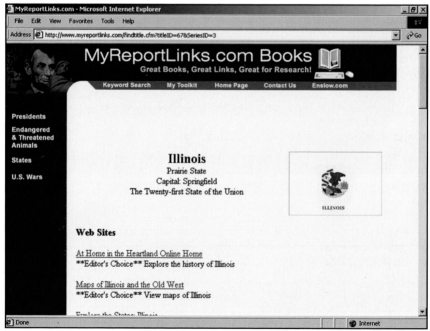

Access:

The Publisher will provide access to the Report Links that back up this book and will try to keep these Report Links up to date on our Web site for three years from the book's first publication date. Please enter **SIL3031** if asked for a password.

> The Internet sites described below can be accessed at
> **http://www.myreportlinks.com**

▶ **At Home in the Heartland Online Home**   *EDITOR'S CHOICE

At this Web site you will find everything, including time lines, maps,
historical biographies, cultural descriptions, and other interesting facts
about the history of Illinois.

Link to this Internet site from http://www.myreportlinks.com

▶ **Maps of Illinois and the Old West**   *EDITOR'S CHOICE

This Web site provides detailed maps that show the changes in
boundaries, cities, and towns throughout the growth of the United
States. You will also find maps of railroads, waterways, steamboats,
and highways.

Link to this Internet site from http://www.myreportlinks.com

▶ **Explore the States: Illinois**   *EDITOR'S CHOICE

America's Story from America's Library, a Library of Congress Web site,
provides basic facts about the state of Illinois, as well as interesting
stories about the history of Illinois.

Link to this Internet site from http://www.myreportlinks.com

▶ **Illinois: A Million Miles from Monday**   *EDITOR'S CHOICE

At this Web site you will find quick facts and figures about the state of
Illinois. You will also find images of the state flag and many useful
links to local newspapers, state museums, and government.

Link to this Internet site from http://www.myreportlinks.com

▶ **Chicago Historical Society's History Files**   *EDITOR'S CHOICE

At this Web site are brief histories about Al Capone, the Chicago
fire, the Chicago Black Sox, and other well-known historic moments
in Chicago history. In addition, this site features many photographs
and illustrations.

Link to this Internet site from http://www.myreportlinks.com

▶ **World's Columbian Exposition:**   *EDITOR'S CHOICE
Idea, Experience, Aftermath

This site offers a comprehensive look into the history and legacy of the
1893 World's Columbian Exposition. Learn about the fair that served
as a gateway to twentieth-century American culture.

Link to this Internet site from http://www.myreportlinks.com

The Internet sites described below can be accessed at
http://www.myreportlinks.com

▶Abraham Lincoln Historical Digitization Project
This site provides a wealth of information about Abraham Lincoln and
Illinois. Read Lincoln's biography and information about his time spent living
in Illinois. Many resources about the history of Illinois are included as well.

Link to this Internet site from http://www.myreportlinks.com

▶The American Presidency: Adlai Ewing Stevenson
At this Web site you will learn about the political life of Adlai Stevenson.
Topics covered in his biography include family life, government service,
presidential campaigns, and his roles as governor of Illinois and ambassador
to the United Nations.

Link to this Internet site from http://www.myreportlinks.com

▶The Art Institute of Chicago Museum
At the Art Institute of Chicago Web site you can explore the institute's
collection and exhibits. You can also read descriptions of the pieces and learn
about the artists. Also featured at this site are video and interactive exhibits.

Link to this Internet site from http://www.myreportlinks.com

▶Black Hawk War of 1832
Beginning with a general overview of the Black Hawk War, this site includes
a biography of Black Hawk, a chief of the Sauk and Fox tribes. Also featured
are American soldiers' accounts of the war, articles, portraits, maps, texts of
treaties, and other related documents.

Link to this Internet site from http://www.myreportlinks.com

▶The Black Press: Soldiers without Swords
This PBS Web site tells the story of the black press and the men and women
responsible for creating a voice for African Americans. In particular, you will
learn about the Chicago Defender, the newspaper that united and educated
African-Americans across the United States.

Link to this Internet site from http://www.myreportlinks.com

▶Building Big
This PBS Web site profiles large structures such as bridges, domes,
skyscrapers, dams, and tunnels around the country. One featured building is
Chicago's Sears Tower. There are many statistics, photographs, and facts about
the world's second-tallest building.

Link to this Internet site from http://www.myreportlinks.com

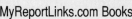
Report Links

 The Internet sites described below can be accessed at
http://www.myreportlinks.com

▶ **Chicago Century of Progress Exposition (World's Fair), 1933–1934**
This PBS Web site focuses on the 1933–34 World's Fair. Exhibits at the fair include diesel engines and stainless steel railroad cars. The fair was a source of optimism for many Americans.

Link to this Internet site from http://www.myreportlinks.com

▶ **Chicago: Historical Information About Chicago**
Compiled by the Chicago Municipal Reference Library, this Web site provides a time line and articles about Chicago history from the city's discovery in 1673 to the 1998 discovery of the Asian longhorned beetle.

Link to this Internet site from http://www.myreportlinks.com

▶ **Chicago: Where Jazz Grew Up**
At this PBS Web site you can explore the history of jazz in Chicago and other places. Here you will find biographies on Louis Armstrong, Joe "King" Oliver, and many others.

Link to this Internet site from http://www.myreportlinks.com

▶ **Discover Illinois**
At this Web site you will learn the history behind Illinois flags and seals, how the Illinois government works, and read facts about Illinois. You will also learn about the state's environment.

Link to this Internet site from http://www.myreportlinks.com

▶ **Grant in Galena**
This Web site provides extensive information about Ulysses S. Grant, including information about his life in Galena, Illinois. A time line of the president's life, individual biographies of Grant's family, and photographs are here as well.

Link to this Internet site from http://www.myreportlinks.com

▶ **Haymarket Affair**
Examine articles, biographies, court transcripts, photographs, and interesting artifacts that relate to the Chicago riots in Haymarket Square in 1886.

Link to this Internet site from http://www.myreportlinks.com

Report Links

The Internet sites described below can be accessed at
http://www.myreportlinks.com

▶ **The History of Chess**
This page features the story of Chess Records. Here you can learn about
the label and its blues artists, including Muddy Waters, Howlin' Wolf,
Little Walter, Jimmy Rogers, Memphis Slim, John Lee Hooker, Sonny Boy
Williamson, Buddy Guy, and more.

Link to this Internet site from http://www.myreportlinks.com

▶ **Illinois**
The official Illinois Web site provides information about living, working, and
visiting Illinois. You will also find links to facts about Illinois and a biography
of the current governor of Illinois.

Link to this Internet site from http://www.myreportlinks.com

▶ **Illinois Historic Preservation Agency—Cahokia Mounds**
Find information about the ancient city of Cahokia, the Cahokia Mounds,
Monks Mound, Illinois American Indian tribes, and more.

Link to this Internet site from http://www.myreportlinks.com

▶ **The Illinois Labor History Society**
At this Web site you can explore the history of the Illinois labor movement
through text, photographs, and other resources.

Link to this Internet site from http://www.myreportlinks.com

▶ **Jane Addams, Her Family, and Hull House**
This online exhibit features biographical information and photographs of
philanthropist, author, and pacifist Jane Addams, founder of Hull House.

Link to this Internet site from http://www.myreportlinks.com .

▶ **Picturing Hemingway: A Writer in His Time**
Ernest Hemingway was born in Oak Park, a suburb of Chicago, Illinois. At
this Web site is a detailed biographical sketch of Hemingway's early life, his
years in Paris, middle years, and later years.

Link to this Internet site from http://www.myreportlinks.com

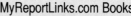
Report Links

 The Internet sites described below can be accessed at
http://www.myreportlinks.com

▶ The Pullman Strike

At this Web site you will learn about the Pullman strike, which began
in Pullman, Illinois, in 1894. The Pullman strike was the first national
strike in United States history, and one of the most important events in
the history of the labor movement.

Link to this Internet site from http://www.myreportlinks.com

▶ Ronald Reagan . . . Tampico, Illinois

The official Ronald Reagan Web site includes a firsthand account of
former President Ronald Reagan's years in Tampico and Dixon, Illinois.

Link to this Internet site from http://www.myreportlinks.com

▶ Stately Knowledge: Illinois

At this Web site you will find facts and figures on the state of Illinois.
You will also find links to additional Internet resources.

Link to this Internet site from http://www.myreportlinks.com

▶ Stephen A. Douglas

Broken up into eight sections, this biography of Stephen Douglas
covers many aspects of his political career, including the debates
between Douglas and Abraham Lincoln.

Link to this Internet site from http://www.myreportlinks.com

▶ Studs Terkel

At this Web page you will find articles about, and interviews with Studs
Terkel, a well-known historian and writer from Chicago.

Link to this Internet site from http://www.myreportlinks.com

▶ U.S. Census Bureau: Illinois

The U.S. Census Bureau Web site provides quick facts about the
state of Illinois. Here you will find statistics on people, business,
and geography.

Link to this Internet site from http://www.myreportlinks.com

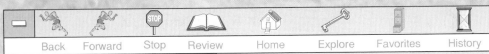

Illinois Facts

Capital
Springfield

Population
12,419,293*

Bird
Cardinal

Tree
White oak

Flower
Purple violet

ILLINOIS

Animal
White-tailed deer

Dance
Square dance

Song
"Illinois"

Motto
State Sovereignty,
National Union.

Slogan
Land of Lincoln

Origin of State's Name
Illinois is the Algonquin
Indian term for "tribe of
superior men."

Gained Statehood
December 3, 1818, the twenty-
first state to enter the Union.

Flag
A bald eagle holds a streamer
bearing the state motto; in the
eagle's claws is a shield with
thirteen bars and thirteen stars
for the original states.

Nickname
The Prairie State

Population reflects the 2000 census.

Land of Lincoln

Illinois sits almost directly in the middle of the United States. It stretches 365 miles from north to south. The distance across the middle of the state from Indiana to Missouri is about half that length. Illinois is one of the top ten states in terms of population.[1]

Until the late nineteenth century, Illinois was an agricultural state. Most people lived on small farms and in

1973 Sears Tower-- World's Tallest Building Until 1996 - Microsoft Internet Explorer

File   Edit   View   Favorites   Tools   Help

Address http://www.chipublib.org/004chicago/timeline/searstower.html   Go

Chicago Timeline

1973 Sears Tower

World's Tallest Building Until 1996

Regains Tallest Occupied Floor Title in 1997

Photo: Chicago Public Library

Chicago became home to the world's tallest building in 1973 when the Sears Tower was topped off. The Sears Tower remained the tallest building in the world until February 13, 1996. The Sears Tower continues to be the tallest building in North America.

Done   Internet

▲ Until 1996, the Sears Tower in Chicago, Illinois, was the tallest building in the world.

small communities. Chicago and Springfield were the largest cities. Today, rural life is rare; most people live in cities, towns, or suburbs.[2]

The northern part of the state is more industrialized than the south.

▶ Chicago: A Major Metropolis

One large city dominates Illinois—Chicago. The greater metropolitan area around Chicago has a population of more than 8 million. Chicago is the third-largest city in the United States. It has large African- and Hispanic-American populations. There are also Irish, Polish, Italian, and Jewish communities. Today these communities are merging.

Many major companies have headquarters in Chicago, and as a result the city contributes a great deal of money to the state treasury. The city also draws a lot of money from the state treasury for transportation, education, welfare, and other state-funded services. Residents of the state's rural areas sometimes resent Chicago's wealth. Still, having a major city is an economic advantage to Illinois as a whole.

▶ Famous Residents: Politicians, Poets, and Musicians

If one city dominates Illinois, one man dominates its history. Abraham Lincoln moved to Illinois as a young man. He lived for several years in New Salem. He was practicing law in Springfield when he was nominated for the presidency. In 1955, the General Assembly, Illinois' legislature, copyrighted the slogan "Land of Lincoln." This means that only Illinois can use this title.

Illinois is famous for other politicians, too. Senator Stephen A. Douglas challenged Lincoln in the famous Lincoln-Douglas debates in 1854. Adlai Stevenson, Jr., once a governor of Illinois, ran for president in 1952 and 1956. He was defeated both times by General Dwight D. Eisenhower, a Republican. In 1960, Stevenson lost the Democratic Party nomination to John F. Kennedy. In 1961, President Kennedy appointed Stevenson ambassador to the United Nations.

Everett Dirksen served six terms in the U.S. House of Representatives. Then he served in the Senate from 1951 until 1968. Dirksen was interested in civil rights and was active in passing legislation to bring equality. He was known for his persuasive speeches.

Ronald Reagan, twice elected president of the United States, was born in Tampico, Illinois. He grew up in Dixon, Illinois.

Richard J. Daley was mayor of Chicago for five terms in a row in the 1950s and 1960s. He was one of the most colorful and powerful mayors of a major American city. An Irishman from the city's stockyards district, Daley was a devoted Democrat. He supported unions and persuaded many voters to choose John F. Kennedy in the 1960

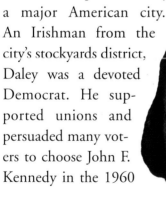

Senator Stephen A. Douglas is perhaps best known for his debates with Abraham Lincoln on the question of slavery.

election. He made friends among various ethnic groups, encouraging them to work together. Daley tried to make sure that "his" city avoided the usual problems of cities faced with rapid growth and inner decay. His son, Richard M. Daley, has also served as mayor of Chicago.

Illinois is known for writers and musicians. Poet Carl Sandburg was born in Galesburg and worked for many years as a journalist in Chicago. Sandburg is perhaps best known for the poem "Chicago." It calls the city the "hog butcher of the world."[3]

Interviewer and author Studs Terkel got people talking and recorded their words in several books. Ernest Hemingway was born in Illinois. So were James Farrell, author of *Studs Lonigan*, and Richard Wright, who wrote about the problems of young African-Americans in ghettos. Jewish novelist Saul Bellow was raised in Chicago, as was African-American poet Gwendolyn Brooks. She was appointed poet laureate of Illinois in 1968.

In the 1920s, Chicago was known for jazz and the blues. Many famous musicians, including Louis Armstrong and Benny Goodman, had their headquarters in the city. Later, singer Frank Sinatra made famous a song that calls Chicago "a toddlin' town."

▶ From the Gold Coast to Galena

A visit to Illinois should begin with the city of Chicago. It is easy to get there. Major highways approach the city from all directions. Planes land at the large and busy O'Hare Airport and at the smaller, older Midway Airport on the city's South Side. Chicago is also the midwestern hub for the Amtrak railroad system.

Chicago has two major museums: the Field Museum of Natural History and the Rosenwald Museum of Science and Industry. The Art Institute of Chicago has a first-class collection of international paintings and artwork from all historical periods. The Shedd Aquarium sits on a finger of land stretching out into Lake Michigan. The Brookfield Zoo is one of the finest zoos in the nation.

Chicago has a large business and shopping area. A ride on the elevated train that circles the original downtown area—called the Loop—is a once-in-a-lifetime experience. North Michigan Avenue is called Chicago's Gold Coast. This strip is just across the Chicago River from the Loop. It offers luxury shopping and dining. Chicago's lakefront has

▲ Chicago, the third largest city in the United States, is located in northeastern Illinois. It is ranked among the world's leading industrial and transportation centers.

man-made beaches in some places and a rocky shoreline in others. Visitors enjoy trips on sightseeing boats on the Chicago River, which circles parts of the Loop. Other attractions include the city's sophisticated atmosphere and many five-star restaurants, such as Morton's of Chicago Steakhouse and Gordon. Old favorites include the Berghoff, which serves sausages and sauerkraut in the heart of downtown.

The city is famous for its architecture and architects. Chicago is the birthplace of the skyscraper. Tourists frequently visit landmark skyscrapers such as the Blackstone Hotel, built in 1908, and the Allerton Hotel, built from 1922 to 1924. The Chicago Board of Trade Building, built in 1930, is important historically even though it has had a new addition. Louis Sullivan was one of Chicago's most famous architects. He designed major buildings at the 1893 Columbian Exposition in Chicago. The city also boasts many residences designed by Frank Lloyd Wright, probably the most famous architect in American history.

About 1.5 million tourists visit the Sears Tower each year. Built in 1973, the 110-story building was the world's tallest until 1996 when the Petronas Towers in Malaysia were built. The Sears Tower houses residences, offices, shopping, and parking.

Unlike many cities, Chicago has two baseball teams. The Cubs play on the North Side at Wrigley Field, one of the oldest classic baseball stadiums in the country. For many years, the late sports announcer Harry Caray led the audience in singing "Take Me Out to the Ball Game" during the seventh-inning stretch. The White Sox play on the South Side at White Sox Park, a new stadium built beside their old Comiskey Park. Chicago's football team, the Bears, and National Basketball Association team, the Bulls, have been with the city for many years, as have the Chicago Blackhawks of the National Hockey League. Chicago also has two professional soccer teams, the Fire of the MLS and the Cobras of the WASL.

Illinois offers many famous places to visit outside Chicago. In Springfield, Abraham Lincoln's home is open to the public. People come from around the world to visit his tomb in the Oak Ridge Cemetery. The library portion of a new Abraham Lincoln Presidential Library and Museum opened in 2002. It houses the largest collection of Lincoln artifacts and documents in the country. The museum portion is scheduled to open in 2004. New Salem, the village where Lincoln lived as a young man, has been reconstructed. It offers a glimpse of life on the frontier in the 1830s.

The home of Ulysses S. Grant in Galena is open to the public. Grant was the Union general who won victory over

▲ The home of former President Ulysses S. Grant is found in Galena, Illinois.

the Confederacy in the Civil War. He is credited with saving the Union. Grant was elected president in 1868 and 1872. The nineteenth-century architecture and atmosphere of Galena have been preserved. You can also take riverboat trips on the Mississippi River at Galena.

Illinois has numerous state parks and recreation areas. The Upper Mississippi National Wildlife and Fish Reserve is in southern Illinois. Starved Rock State Park, located on the Illinois River, offers views of an unusual geological formation and a bit of history. The huge rock was home to the Illiniwek Indians, a subtribe of the Kaskaskia. In a battle, Potowatomis surrounded the Illiniwek. Isolated on

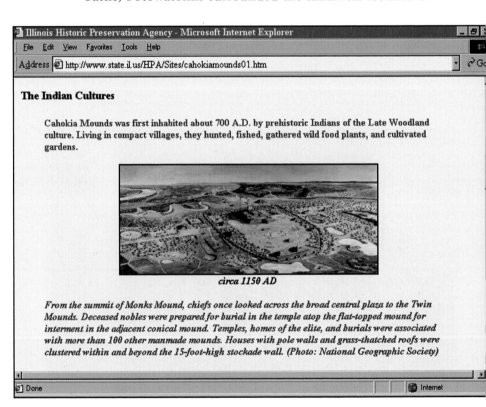

The Cahokia Mounds are the largest known American Indian mounds in the United States. Archaeologists estimate that the city of Cahokia was inhabited from about A.D. 700 to A.D. 1400.

the rock, the Illiniwek died of starvation. Father Jacques Marquette, an early French explorer, established a mission there. The French later built Fort St. Louis on the top of the rock.

Monks Mound in Cahokia Mounds State Park is the largest prehistoric earthen mound in the Americas. American Indians used these mounds for ceremonial burials and for storage. Protective walls and a circle of stones resemble Stonehenge in England. The Cahokia Mounds are sometimes called Wood Henge.[4] Unfortunately, many mounds were destroyed when farmers plowed the fields.

Chapter 2

Land and Climate

Illinois is called the Prairie State because two thirds of its land was once grassland prairie. This flat or gently rolling region is known as the Central Plains. In the 1600s, American Indians hunted buffalo on the prairie. The land also boasted deer, wild game birds, and small animals, such as squirrels, opossums, rabbits, and prairie dogs. Early explorers sold furs from the plentiful beavers on the rivers. By the time settlers pushed into the territory, the buffalo had moved westward but other game remained.

▶ A State of Many Landscapes

Plowing and planting have broken up much of the original prairie. Trees were cut for log homes, rail fences, railroad ties, and lumber. Today, only a few thousand acres of prairie grasslands have been preserved. Rare and endangered species of birds and animals nest and breed there. About 1,000 acres of virgin forest also have been protected from development.

In the northwest, the land is hilly. Bluffs border the Mississippi River. The Shawnee Hills, also known as the Illinois Ozarks, stretch across the southern part of the state. In the far south lies the northern tip of the Gulf Coastal Plain, a flat region that stretches north from the Gulf of Mexico.

The northern two thirds of the state has rich, black soil left from the days of the prairie. In the southern third, the soil is sandier and not as good for growing crops.

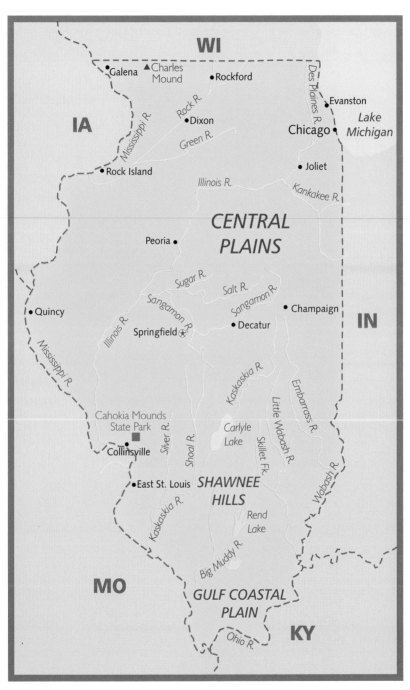

△ A map of Illinois.

▷ Climate

The climate in Illinois varies greatly from north to south. The northern border of the state is at the latitude of Boston, Massachusetts. The southern tip is about on a line with Norfolk, Virginia. The growing season in the north is a month shorter than in the south.

Winters in the north can be bitter. Temperatures often fall below freezing. Occasionally they dip to near zero. Northwestern Illinois averages thirty-five days of snowfall a year. The southeastern end of the state averages only five. Snowfall in the growing or harvesting seasons can hurt the state's agriculture. Severe or long-lasting snowfall in the north disrupts transportation, trade, and communications. In the winter of 1977–78, a record blizzard blocked

▲ The weather in Chicago (shown here) is usually normal for the season. However, winds off of nearby Lake Michigan can change the temperature within minutes.

highways, killed cattle and people, closed schools and buildings, and resulted in great economic loss.[1]

Summers in Illinois can be as hot as the winters are cold. The temperature often reaches more than 100°F in Chicago. Yet when the wind shifts and brings breezes off Lake Michigan, the temperature can drop dramatically. Along the Mississippi River and in southern Illinois, there are no cooling breezes to break the heat. Summers are hot and humid.

Natural Disasters

Illinois is not part of "Tornado Alley," which stretches across Texas, Kansas, and Oklahoma. Still, tornados do occur. One devastating tornado crossed Illinois in March 1925. It was on the ground for more than 200 miles and killed 695 people, both national records.[2]

Earthquakes are also not common, but can happen. The large Madrid fault system runs under southern Illinois. Severe earthquakes shook much of the middle of the United States in 1811. Aftershocks continued for weeks. Another major earthquake was recorded in January 1812.[3]

Flooding is a more frequent problem than drought. The Mississippi River is on the western border of the state. The Ohio River borders the lower third of Illinois. The two rivers meet at the southern tip of the state, near Cairo (pronounced "care-oh"). The Illinois River cuts across the center of the state, flowing southwest from Chicago to enter the Mississippi near St. Louis, Missouri. Smaller rivers and streams crisscross the state. Almost all of them have experienced major floods. Sometimes floods are caused when man-made structures—bridges, canals, and dikes—disrupt the natural flow of water.

Economy

Agriculture is no longer the center of Illinois' economy. In 1910, there were 253,000 farms in the state. In 2001, there were 76,000. Yet the state is still one of the world's leading suppliers of field corn, feeder hogs, and soybeans. Soybeans replaced cotton as the major crop in southern

Debsweb2 - Microsoft Internet Explorer

File Edit View Favorites Tools Help

Address http://www.cc.ukans.edu/kansas/pullman/texts/debs.html

Eugene Victor Debs

(1855-1926)

Eugene Victor Debs was born on November 5, 1855 in Terre Haute, Indiana. Eugene was one of six surviving children and the first born son. His parents owned a small grocery store that was in one of the front rooms of their two-story home. The Deb's household fostered an intellectual spirit that grew within Eugene Debs. At the age of fourteen Debs left school to become a paint scraper for the Terre Haute and Indianapolis Railroad. Debs found his calling amongst the rail-workers, which was to be the champion of industrial workers everywhere in the United States. His career would span some of the most turbulent times in American labor history, and he would leave a legacy of tenacious fighter for the common man and the good of all.

After returning to Terre Haute, because his family was worried about his safety, while working for the Railroad. He started working as a warehouse worker for a friend of his father. It was while he was working in the warehouse that Debs and a group of his friends founded the Occidental Literary Club. His participation in this club was to prove fundamental to his development as a labor leader. This was because Eugene Debs had many popular speakers at the club, including Wendell Phillips and Susan B. Anthony. It was the exposure to these types of speakers that Debs' increasing literary skills, which enabled him to become an effective member in the Vigo Lodge of the Locomotive Firemen (BLF).

Even though Deb's was not a railroad employee he had joined the BLF because of his increasing interest in labor issues. He started serving as a labor organizer and secretary for the brotherhood. Then in 1876 he became active in the BLF national conventions as well as writing articles for the Brotherhood of Locomotive Firemen's Magazine. In addition to this, between the

Done   Internet

▲ In 1893, Eugene Victor Debs founded the American Railway Union (ARU). The Pullman Strike, also known as the Chicago Strike, occurred in 1894. Members of the ARU sympathized with the Pullman employees, and refused to haul railroad cars made by the Pullman company.

Illinois in the 1960s. The production and sale of foodstuffs accounted for about 25 percent of the state's exports as late as the 1980s.[1]

▶ Transportation

Farmers have always benefited from Illinois' excellent transportation system. Before the 1850s, water was the main means of transporting farm products. In 1836, work began on a canal to connect the Illinois River to Lake Michigan. This canal would make it possible to move goods by water all the way from Montreal to New Orleans. Engineering and financial difficulties delayed completion of the canal for many years. It finally opened in the late 1840s. By that time, however, the railroad had arrived. The Illinois Central Railroad was chartered in 1851 to go from Cairo, at the southern tip of the state, to Galena, in the far northwestern corner. Today, it is the only major rail carrier in the United States still operating under its own name 150 years after it began.

▶ Industry

For more than 150 years, coal mining was an important industry. Illinois has one of the largest bituminous, or soft, coal fields in the United States. Soft coal is dry, smokeless, cheap and heats quickly. Most mines in Illinois are strip or surface mines rather than underground shafts. Strip-mining disturbs the land because an open pit is dug in the surface.

Mining is less profitable today because of laws that restrict the use of coal. These laws were passed to keep the air clean. Since the early 1970s, mining companies have also been forced to restore the landscape after strip-mining.

Back | Forward | Stop | Review | Home | Explore | Favorites | History

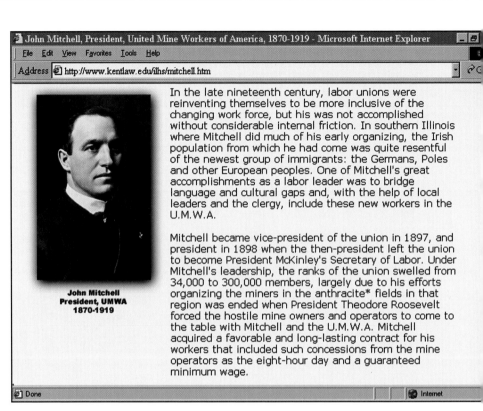

John Mitchell, President, United Mine Workers of America, 1870-1919 - Microsoft Internet Explorer

File   Edit   View   Favorites   Tools   Help

Address http://www.kentlaw.edu/ilhs/mitchell.htm

John Mitchell
President, UMWA
1870-1919

In the late nineteenth century, labor unions were reinventing themselves to be more inclusive of the changing work force, but his was not accomplished without considerable internal friction. In southern Illinois where Mitchell did much of his early organizing, the Irish population from which he had come was quite resentful of the newest group of immigrants: the Germans, Poles and other European peoples. One of Mitchell's great accomplishments as a labor leader was to bridge language and cultural gaps and, with the help of local leaders and the clergy, include these new workers in the U.M.W.A.

Mitchell became vice-president of the union in 1897, and president in 1898 when the then-president left the union to become President McKinley's Secretary of Labor. Under Mitchell's leadership, the ranks of the union swelled from 34,000 to 300,000 members, largely due to his efforts organizing the miners in the anthracite* fields in that region was ended when President Theodore Roosevelt forced the hostile mine owners and operators to come to the table with Mitchell and the U.M.W.A. Mitchell acquired a favorable and long-lasting contract for his workers that included such concessions from the mine operators as the eight-hour day and a guaranteed minimum wage.

Done   Internet

▲ *John Mitchell became president of the United Mine Workers of America in 1898.*

By 1999, only ten thousand people were employed in the mining industry in Illinois.

Meatpacking was a major industry in Chicago in the late nineteenth century. Armour and Swift and other major meatpackers were located near the Union Stock Yards on the city's West Side. Chicago was called "Slaughterhouse to the World." After World War II, refrigerated transportation made it possible for companies to move to less expensive, rural areas. The Union Stock Yards officially closed in 1971.

Major industries in Illinois today are machinery, food processing, electric equipment, chemical products, printing and publishing, fabricated metal production, transportation equipment, petroleum, and coal. Tourism has also become vital to the state's economy.

▶ "Illinois First"

The state faces common problems: traffic, few open spaces, pollution, and the decay of its older inner cities. Illinois has created a program called "Illinois First" to help solve these problems, by giving grants to local governments and small businesses. The state provides money for police, firefighters, roads, and sewer and water systems. It also supports youth and senior citizen programs, parks and playgrounds, schools, colleges, and universities. The state works to fix up downtown areas and preserve historic streets and buildings. Illinois has its eye on the past—and on tomorrow.

▲ Traffic congestion on Chicago's bustling Michigan Avenue Bridge is a daily inconvenience for most commuters.

Chapter 4

Government

The structure of the Illinois government resembles that of the United States federal government. The legislature is called the General Assembly. It consists of a senate and a house of representatives. Two representatives and one senator are elected from each of the fifty-nine districts.[1] Each house elects a majority and a minority leader.

▲ *The state capitol building in Springfield, Illinois.*

The governor is the chief executive and holds strong powers. He or she appoints all officers who are not elected, after receiving the approval of the General Assembly. The governor can call a special session of the assembly and can adjourn the assembly if necessary. The authority of the governor has increased steadily with such national crises as the Civil War.[2]

The lieutenant governor must belong to the same political party as the governor. The governor and the lieutenant governor run for election together. Other elected officials are the attorney general, secretary of state, comptroller, and treasurer.

Illinois has three levels of courts: the Supreme Court, Appellate (appeals) Court, and Circuit Courts. The Supreme Court is the state's highest court.

The General Assembly controls local governments, except for Chicago and the state's 102 counties. Illinois has more than six thousand local units of government, including counties, towns and cities, school districts, hospital districts, and water and sewage districts.[3]

In 2000, Illinois also had twenty members in the U.S. House of Representatives and held twenty-two electoral votes.

▶ Constitutional Conventions

Illinois has had four constitutional conventions. The first met in Kaskaskia in August 1818 to prepare for statehood. The strongest debate was over the issue of slavery. The constitution, which did not allow slavery, was accepted by the U.S. Congress. A second constitution was approved in 1848. It still did not approve slavery. Other changes were not significant.

A constitution approved in 1870 limited the General Assembly to dealing with public matters. It was not allowed to make laws about private matters, such as lawsuits, debts, adoption, and so forth. The word "white" was deleted from the voting rights article, but the word "male" remained. This meant black men could now vote, but any woman still could not.

The next constitutional convention was not called for almost a hundred years. The constitution of 1969 gave the governor more power. Cities with a population of twenty-five thousand or more were given more control over their affairs. This control is called home rule.[4]

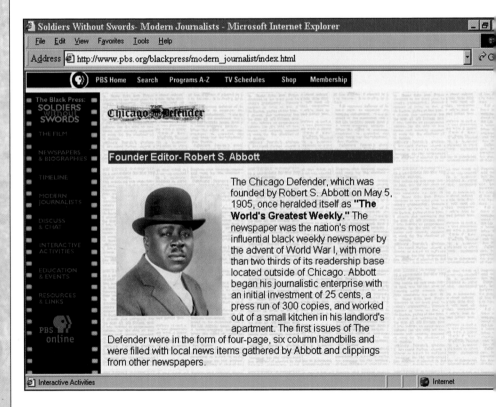

▲ Despite Illinois' mixed record on racial equality, Robert S. Abbott founded the Chicago Defender, one of the nation's largest and most influential black newspapers, in 1905.

The Illinois population is almost evenly divided between Republicans and Democrats. Chicago and the southern counties tend to vote Democrat. The rapidly growing suburbs around Chicago usually vote Republican. In national elections, major candidates campaign hard in Illinois, because it is a "swing state," meaning the vote can swing to either party. Both sides have a good chance of winning an election.

▶ Equal Rights

Illinois has a mixed record on racial and women's equality. Women were admitted to colleges and universities in the late nineteenth century. In 1920, Illinois was the first state east of the Mississippi to allow women to vote.[5] Illinois, though, was also one of the states that did not ratify the Equal Rights Amendment in the late twentieth century.

Illinois Senator Everett Dirksen fought for civil rights on a national level and in his state. Chicago elected its first woman mayor, Jane Byrne, and its first African-American mayor, Harold Washington, in the 1980s.

Chapter 5

History

Burial mounds in central Illinois suggest that the American Indians settled there as early as five thousand years ago. These prehistoric natives had disappeared by about A.D. 1500. The remaining tribes were called Illiniwek by the early European explorers.

▶ Early Explorers

The first Europeans to explore the territory were French. In the 1670s, Louis Joliet and Father Jacques Marquette followed the Mississippi River to the south. Joliet hoped to find a continuous waterway from Montreal to the Gulf of Mexico. Marquette wanted to convert the natives to Christianity. Hostile American Indians forced them to turn back. On their trip north, they reached a land they called "prairie" or "large meadow" in French. Marquette spent the winter at the mouth of the Chicago River.

In the early 1680s, René-Robert Cavelier, also called Sieur de La Salle, explored the lower Mississippi and built Fort Crèvecoeur near present-day Peoria. On his second trip to Illinois, La Salle reached the mouth of the Mississippi and claimed all land surrounding the river in the name of France. Illinois thus became French territory.

▶ Revolutionary Period

In 1763, the British won the French and Indian War. During this conflict, France and England fought for territory in

North America. Many American Indian tribes sided with the French. After Britain's victory, the French government abandoned Illinois and the Northwest Territory. The Northwest Territory consisted of portions of present-day Ohio, Illinois, Michigan, Indiana, Wisconsin, and Minnesota. Small French colonies remained in Illinois.

During the Revolutionary War, the British were in control of much of the Northwest Territory, including Illinois. American Indians sided with the British. A small unit of the revolutionary army defeated the British troops in Illinois. French settlers who still lived at Kaskaskia helped the revolutionaries.[1] When the Revolutionary War ended, the region became a colony of Virginia. In 1784, Virginia gave the land to the United States government.

There was some new settlement in the area. In the 1780s, Jean Baptiste Point du Sable established a trading post at the mouth of the Chicago River. It was the first permanent establishment in Chicago.

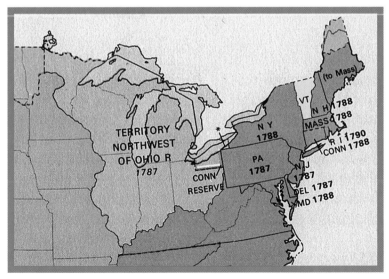

▲ Illinois had been part of the Northwest Territory, shown here in blue.

Early Statehood

In 1817, legislator Nathaniel Pope convinced Congress to grant statehood to the Illinois territory. He also persuaded the legislature that the new state should include sixty miles of Lake Michigan shoreline.

When Illinois became a state, most of its residents lived along the rivers in the southern part of the state. They were frontiersmen from Kentucky and Tennessee. Many had little education, and they were often prejudiced against African Americans. Illinois never allowed slavery, but the state had laws to prevent slaves from escaping through Illinois.

Illinois's second governor, Edward Coles, was a former plantation owner who freed his slaves when he moved to Illinois. When the legislature wanted to make slavery legal in 1819, Coles led the abolitionists (the group of people who wished to end slavery). In 1824, the voters sided with the abolitionists.[2]

Black Hawk's War

Several American Indian tribes still occupied Illinois at the time of statehood. They were mostly of the Sauk and Fox tribes. They were ordered to cross the river into present-day Missouri.

A chief named Black Hawk refused to go. In 1831, Illinois militia and federal troops drove Black Hawk's people across the Mississippi. Black Hawk returned in 1832 to lead his men on raids throughout the countryside, burning homes and scalping settlers. What happened to end Black Hawk's rebellion is not clear. Some say he either surrendered to a government representative or was betrayed by

Black Hawk War of 1832 - Microsoft Internet Explorer

File Edit View Favorites Tools Help

Address http://lincoln.lib.niu.edu/blackhawk/index.html   Go

The Black Hawk War of 1832

- Home
- Primary Materials
- Interpretive Materials
- Maps and Images
- Related Sites
- Lincoln/Net

In May of 1832 Sac and Fox Indians under the leadership of Black Hawk left the Iowa territory and returned to their homes across the Mississippi River in northern Illinois. These Native Americans had lost their Illinois lands in a disputed treaty signed in St. Louis in 1805. Their return to northern Illinois sparked widespread panic among white settlers, and Illinois Governor Reynolds quickly called up the militia, which included a young Abraham Lincoln.

Both the militia and regular army troops proved unable to locate the elusive Indians at first, but by July they had begun to pursue Black Hawk's band across northern Illinois and southwestern Wisconsin, engaging them in a major conflict at Wisconsin Heights before finally routing the Indians at Bad Axe on the Mississippi River.

▲Top

Done   Internet

▲ *In the Black Hawk War of 1832, the Sauk and Fox Indians tried unsuccessfully to regain one of their villages.*

members of the Winnebago tribe in exchange for twenty horses and a hundred dollars.[3]

Mormon Refugees

In 1839, Mormon leader Brigham Young brought five thousand followers to Illinois. They were escaping persecution in Missouri. The Mormons settled in Nauvoo, on the Mississippi River about seventy miles north of Quincy. By 1842, the independent Mormons had formed their own courts and militia. Nauvoo was never prosperous, but by 1845 it was the largest city in Illinois, with twelve thousand residents.

Most Illinois citizens opposed polygamy, or multiple marriages, which the Mormons practiced. The Mormons were also accused of making counterfeit money and other criminal activities. The local government feared that mobs would attack the Mormons. In 1844, Joseph Smith, founder of the Mormon religion, was jailed for his own protection in Carthage, eighteen miles from Nauvoo. A mob stormed the jail and killed Smith and his brother. By 1846, most Mormons had left Illinois for Utah.

▶ Growing Prosperity

In the 1850s, railroads attracted large industries, such as storage companies for grain, coal, and stone. The meat-packing companies of Swift and Armour set up business in Chicago. So did the Kimball piano company. Agricultural improvements, such as John Deere's steel plow and Cyrus McCormick's mass-produced reaper, made farmers more efficient. Illinois was prospering. Then came the Civil War.

▶ Civil War

In 1860, Lincoln was elected president. He ran on the ticket of the new Republican Party. The people of Illinois supported Lincoln and the Union. Even southern counties responded to the call for soldiers. Illinois sent almost 260,000 men to battle; nearly 35,000 died.[4]

▶ The Great Chicago Fire

After the Civil War, Illinois, and particularly Chicago, prospered. Then on October 9, 1871, the Chicago fire bell sounded three times, signaling a fire in the third ward—the city's West Side. The fire began in the barn belonging to a family named O'Leary. Winds from the west carried the flames. The fire quickly spread and destroyed the

▲ *Lincoln with his advisors during the Civil War. From left to right are Gen. William T. Sherman, Gen. Ulysses S. Grant, Lincoln and Adm. David Porter.*

business section of Chicago. The flames jumped the Chicago River and also burned much of the North Side.

The city burned for more than twenty-four hours. An estimated 300 people died in the fire, although only 120 bodies were ever found. About eighteen thousand buildings were destroyed.

The West Side and the South Side of the city were mostly untouched. The stockyards and grain elevators still stood. The city began to rebuild almost immediately, and Chicago doubled its population in the 1870s.

▷ Labor Unrest

As industry grew, owners made more demands of their employees. Workers at the McCormick plant in Chicago

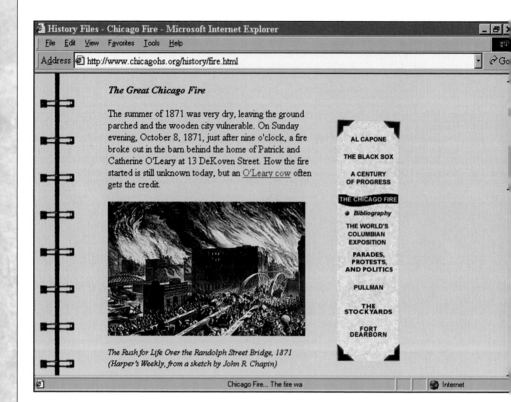

History Files - Chicago Fire - Microsoft Internet Explorer

File Edit View Favorites Tools Help

Address http://www.chicagohs.org/history/fire.html

The Great Chicago Fire

The summer of 1871 was very dry, leaving the ground parched and the wooden city vulnerable. On Sunday evening, October 8, 1871, just after nine o'clock, a fire broke out in the barn behind the home of Patrick and Catherine O'Leary at 13 DeKoven Street. How the fire started is still unknown today, but an O'Leary cow often gets the credit.

AL CAPONE

THE BLACK SOX

A CENTURY OF PROGRESS

THE CHICAGO FIRE

● Bibliography

THE WORLD'S COLUMBIAN EXPOSITION

PARADES, PROTESTS, AND POLITICS

PULLMAN

THE STOCKYARDS

FORT DEARBORN

The Rush for Life Over the Randolph Street Bridge, 1871 (Harper's Weekly, from a sketch by John R. Chapin)

Chicago Fire... The fire wa   Internet

In 1871, a fire broke out and destroyed most of the North Side of the city. Today it is known as the Great Chicago Fire.

and in other industries rebelled against long hours and low pay. In southern Illinois, United Mine Workers went on strike over unsafe conditions. Strikers throughout the state demanded an eight-hour workday.

The most violent uprising was the Haymarket Riot in Chicago. Anarchists (people seeking to overthrow the existing system of government and business) had been protesting working conditions at the McCormick plant. On May 4, 1886, the anarchists gathered at Haymarket Square. The police ordered the crowd to break up. Someone threw a bomb, killing seven police officers. The police opened fire on the fleeing men, killing one. Several prominent anarchists were arrested, and four were later hanged.

▶ Hull House

The immigrants who poured into the Chicago area also faced problems. They needed adequate living and working conditions. In the 1880s, a wealthy woman named Jane Addams established Hull House. It was a kind of community center in the slums of Chicago's West Side. Hull House helped immigrants adjust to life in America. At first, Hull House staff educated kindergartners. Eventually, they developed programs that helped people through college extension classes. Hull House offered immigrant women a social life. They learned how to survive in a world very different from their homelands. Many women of influence and wealth volunteered at Hull House.

▶ Growth and Fame

In spite of labor troubles and poor immigrants, Chicago became more sophisticated. In 1893, the city hosted the Columbian Exposition, perhaps the most influential world's fair ever held. Sculptors, artists, authors, and historians of world fame came to Chicago. Bill Hickok set up his Wild West show just outside the fairgrounds. George Washington Ferris built his first Ferris wheel for the event.

By the 1890s, Illinois was among the leading industrial states. Growth caused problems, though, such as water pollution. There were also accusations that spoiled meat was shipped from Chicago's packinghouses. Upton Sinclair's book *The Jungle* exposed the meatpacking industry to a horrified nation.

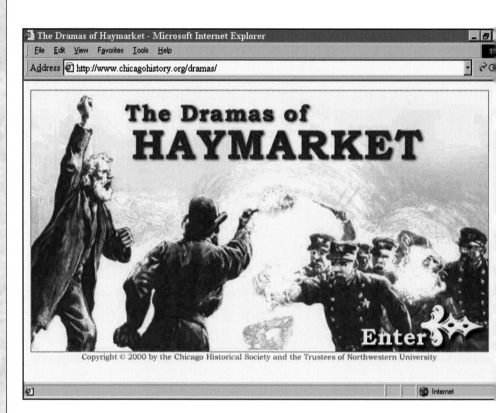

The Dramas of Haymarket - Microsoft Internet Explorer

File   Edit   View   Favorites   Tools   Help

Address http://www.chicagohistory.org/dramas/

The Dramas of
HAYMARKET

Enter

Internet

The Haymarket Riot occurred in 1886, when a group of workers held a meeting in Haymarket Square in Chicago to protest police actions against strikers at the McCormick industrial plant.

▶ The Early Twentieth Century

The early 1900s brought improvements in transportation. In the nineteenth century, farmers could only travel to town or visit relatives by horse and buggy. After 1900, an electric train system increased travel in rural areas. After 1925, people began to travel by automobile. By 1927, approximately 90 percent of residents of rural southern Illinois owned cars.[5] The installation of telephones also made rural areas less isolated.

In Chicago, public transportation changed working people's lives. Families could live in pleasant neighborhoods five or ten miles from downtown.

New federal laws were passed to improve working conditions. Major companies, such as International Harvester, Western Electric, U.S. Steel, and the meatpackers, installed safety devices and clean rest rooms. They provided pensions and death benefits for employees.

Illinois saw a great deal of violence during the early 1900s. Dozens were killed and hundreds injured in race riots in Springfield in 1908, East St. Louis in 1917, and Chicago in 1919. At the coalfields in Herrin, more than

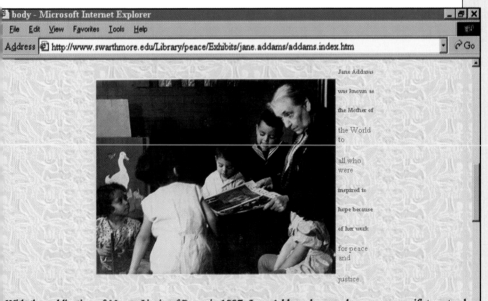

body - Microsoft Internet Explorer

File   Edit   View   Favorites   Tools   Help

Address http://www.swarthmore.edu/Library/peace/Exhibits/jane.addams/addams.index.htm   Go

Jane Addams was known as the Mother of the World to all who were inspired to hope because of her work for peace and justice.

With the publication of *Newer Ideals of Peace* in 1907, Jane Addams became known as a pacifist, a stand which brought her much ridicule and censure when the United States finally entered World War I. Yet by 1931, public opinion had swayed to embrace her ideas and that year she was awarded the Nobel Peace Prize, shared with Nicholas Murray Butler. By then, her reputation as the Mother of the World was firmly established. She received letters from people around the world not only praising her for her

Done   Internet

▲ In the 1880s, Jane Addams established Hull House in Chicago. It was designed to help immigrant women and children adjust to life in America.

twenty people died in a clash between striking miners and strikebreakers.

▶ Organized Crime

Chicago, East St. Louis, and mining towns also saw the development of organized crime. In the early 1900s, selling liquor was illegal. This law was called Prohibition. Crime organizations profited from trading in illegal liquor. Al Capone was Chicago's most notorious gangster. He came to Chicago from New York to run the crime organization. Capone gained great wealth and strong influence by having his enemies killed. Eventually, he was jailed for tax evasion.

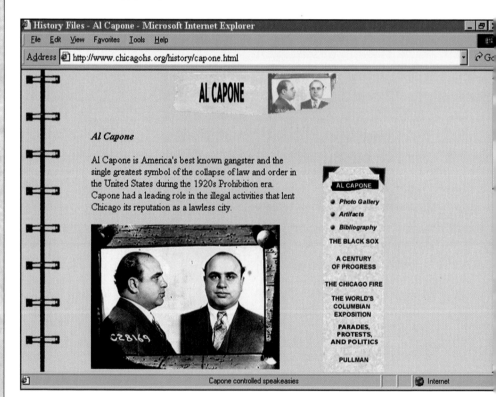

▲ Al Capone was one of America's most powerful gangsters.

Gang warfare was common. The most frightening example was the St. Valentine's Day Massacre of 1929. Six members of Bugs Moran's gang were gunned down on Chicago's North Clark Street.

World War I

At the outbreak of World War I, Illinois was the center of the German-American population. Germany was the United States' chief enemy in the war, and Chicago had the highest number of German residents. Germans also lived in northern rural areas and in such towns as Peoria and Kankakee. Twenty-five German-Americans from Illinois traveled to Washington, D.C. They wanted to persuade President Woodrow Wilson that the United States should not make declare against Germany.[6]

When the United States entered the war on April 6, 1917, however, Illinois was united against the enemy. The state became a training ground for land, sea, and air force troops. Illinois sent more than 314,000 men to war.

The Depression and World War II

The Great Depression began with the fall of the stock market in October 1929. Farmers had overproduced and were in financial trouble even before the Depression. Now miners were idle, and one fourth of all factory workers were out of a job. The decline in tax payments meant the state of Illinois was in financial difficulty.

The General Assembly reduced property taxes, created a sales tax, and established the Illinois Emergency Relief Commission to feed and shelter the jobless. Conditions improved by the late 1930s. World War II and government welfare programs brought the country—and Illinois—out of the Depression.

Illinois sent 958,000 men and 14,000 women to World War II. Of these, 24,000 died. Illinois factories began producing military equipment. Atomic research programs started during the war. Major work was done in a laboratory at the University of Chicago's Stagg Field.[7]

The 1960s

There was new civil unrest during the peace movement of the 1960s. The General Assembly was reluctant to pass civil rights legislation. In 1966, Martin Luther King, Jr., walked the streets of Chicago in protest. After his assassination in 1968, African-American Chicagoans rioted for several days.

The Democratic National Convention was held in Chicago that year. Peace protesters demonstrated against the Vietnam War, racial discrimination, and the advantages of the wealthy. Mayor Daley ordered the police to break up the protests. They did, using clubs and tear gas.

Ahead to the Future

In the 1990s, Illinois faced several challenges. The state was losing jobs, industries, and people. With industries leaving the state, many workers were unemployed. Miners were losing their jobs because industries were using less coal. The environment also needed attention.

With the 1999 election of Governor George H. Ryan, the state's fortunes seemed on the rise. Governor Ryan created new programs to meet the state's problems. In his 2001 "State of the State" address, he said the business world was taking notice of Illinois. The unemployment rate was the lowest in a generation. A $95 million program was fighting pollution. Ryan proudly claimed that Illinois in 2001 was better and more prosperous than in 1999, and it would get even better.[8]

Chapter Notes

Chapter 1. Land of Lincoln

1. David Kenney and Barbara Brown, *Basic Illinois Government: A Systematic Explanation* (Carbondale: Southern Illinois University Press, 1993), p. 4.

2. A. Doyne Horsley, *Illinois: A Geography* (Boulder, Colo.: Westview Press, 1986), pp. 195–196.

3. Carl Sandburg, "Chicago," *The Academy of American Poets*, n.d., <http://www.poets.org/poems/poemprnt.cfm?prmID=1033> (August 14, 2002).

4 Horsley, p. 29.

Chapter 2. Land and Climate

1. A. Doyne Horsley, *Illinois: A Geography* (Boulder, Colo.: Westview Press, 1986), p. 79.

2. Ibid., p. 78.

3. Robert P. Howard, *Illinois: A History of the Prairie State* (Grand Rapids, Mich.: William B. Eerdman's Publishing Company, 1972), p. 80.

Chapter 3. Economy

1. A. Doyne Horsley, *Illinois: A Geography* (Boulder, Colo.: Westview Press, 1986), p. 3.

Chapter 4. Government

1. David Kenney and Barbara Brown, *Basic Illinois Government: A Systematic Explanation* (Carbondale: Southern Illinois University Press, 1993), p. 78.

2. Ibid., p. 81.

3. Ibid., p. 142.

4. Lois A. Carrier, *Illinois: Crossroads of a Continent* (Urbana: University of Illinois Press, 1993), p. 247.

5. Ibid., p. 253.

Chapter 5. History

1. Robert P. Howard, *Illinois: A History of the Prairie State* (Grand Rapids, Mich.: William B. Eerdman's Publishing Company, 1972), pp. 50–53.

2. Ibid., pp. 133–137.

3. Paula Mitchell Marks, *In a Barren Land: American Indian Dispossession and Survival* (New York: William Morrow and Company, 1998), p. 65; and Dee Brown, *Bury My Heart at Wounded Knee* (New York: Holt, Rinehart & Winston, 1970), p. 5.

4. Howard, p. 298.

5. Richard J. Jensen, *Illinois: A History* (New York: W. W. Norton and Company, 1978), p. 91.

6. Ibid., p. 438.

7. Lois A. Carrier, *Illinois: Crossroads of a Continent* (Urbana: University of Illinois Press, 1993), p. 222.

8. George H. Ryan, "State of the State Address for 2001," *IL 2001*, January 31, 2001, <http//www.state.il.us/gov/sosspeach.htm> (July 24, 2002).

Further Reading

Alter, Judy. *Abraham Lincoln.* Berkeley Heights, N.J.: MyReportLinks.com Books, 2002.

Boekhoff, P.M. and Stuart A. Kallen. *Illinois.* Farmington Hills, Mich.: Gale Group, 2001.

Feeley, Kathleen. *Illinois: The Prairie State.* Milwaukee: Gareth Stevens Inc., 2002.

Fowler, Allan. *Illinois.* Danbury, Conn.: Children's Press, 1999.

Fradin, Dennis Brindell. *Illinois.* Danbury, Conn.: Children's Press, 1991.

Jensen, Richard J. *Illinois: A History.* Champaign/Urbana: University of Illinois Press, 2001.

Joseph, Paul. *Illinois.* Edina, Minn.: ABDO Publishing Company, 1998.

Santella, Andrew. *Illinois,* 2nd ed., Danbury, Conn.: Children's Press, 1998.

Somervill, Barbara A. *Illinois.* Danbury, Conn.: Children's Press, 2001.

Sullivan, George E. *Abraham Lincoln.* New York: Scholastic, Inc., 2001.